Cross Shaped Space

A Book of Prayers

© Sanctus Media Ltd 2011

Published by Astwood Publishing
Website: www.astwood.org.uk

ISBN 978-0-9566732-2-0

Created, Designed and Typeset by:
Sanctus Media Ltd
Grahamsdyke Avenue
Bo'ness
EH51 9DT

Tel: 01506 827217
Website: www.sanctusmedia.com

Printed by:
Bell & Bain Ltd
303 Burnfield Road
Thornliebank
Glagow
G46 7UQ

Tel: 0141-649 5697
Website: www.bell-bain.com

Images and Photography:
www.shutterstock.com
Marcus Ford

Preface

This book of prayers prepares us for Easter and Pentecost as we move through Lent. We have chosen as our theme the "Cross Shaped Space". I'm indebted to Peter Gardner, one of our contributors, for giving us the stimulus to develop this theme. A few years ago I visited his church to find a huge square piece of material with a cross shaped space in its centre. It was this depiction that inspired the material for the liturgy of the cross shaped space. This material can be viewed at www.sanctuaryfirst.org.uk

When we centre our thoughts around the cross we engage with the gifts and the graces of God through the power of the Holy Spirit. There is much that we can learn from this cross shaped space. It is interesting that in John's Gospel the death of Jesus is recorded in such a way that it involves Jesus "giving up his Spirit". Take a moment to look up John 19:30, as Christ breathed his last and gave up the Spirit he breathed the Spirit out into the world. You might say into the hearts of believers. It is from the cross and through the cross that we encounter the gifts and the fruit of the Holy Spirit in our lives.

The cross shaped space invites us to fit ourselves on the cross: to walk through the cross; to make a daily cross shaped space in our lives; to experience the power of the resurrection through the suffering of the cross.

The cross shaped space we believe can be an important visual to draw us closer to God.

These prayers engage with the consequences of all who seek to live in the cross shaped space. What does it mean to take our working life and fit it into the cross shaped space? What does it mean to enter into life through the cross and receive the gifts of the Holy Spirit? What does it mean to walk through the cross into the world and live out the fruit of the Spirit? What does it mean to understand and engage with the life of the Spirit that is at work in the world?

Albert Bogle
Bo'ness 2011

sanctuaryfirst
A PLACE TO BE

www.sanctuaryfirst.org.uk

Contents

Like children 8
Commitment 9
Political 10
How long? 11
iDisciples... 12
Discipleship diversions 13
The plans... 14
Lord of the cross 15
Why did she weep?.. 16
That's what Lent is about 17
Questions 18
Suffering servant 19
It is finished... 20
The crucified poor 21
Saved by a prayer 22
Crucifixion hasn't changed 23
God forsaken 24
I can't believe 25
Out of sight.. 26
New day 27
Promise 28
Nonsense talk 29
Error 404 30
The gardener God 31
Poor Thomas 32
Sorry, a bit late 33
The turn of a coin 34
Resurrection is not on the agenda 35
Sorry Lord, we're so 36
A touch of doubt 37
Doubters anonymous 38
Work as worship 39
Valuing others 40
The death of a colleague 41
Working with all my heart 42
Feeling rejected 43
Why this job? 44
Work – God wants the best for me! 45
I'm not moving 46
Your man in Havana? 47
Joy 48
Patience 49
Peace 50
Goodness 51
Kindness and gentleness 52
Self-control 53
The teacher.. 54
The liberator 55
The guide 56
Loose talk 57
All my days 58
View from the cross 59
I don't fit in 60
Chill out 61

Like children

Lord,
I saw You were busy
with some beginners last night,
I think You were talking to them
about basic stuff,
You know,
basic discipleship.
They looked like children.
I joined the group for a little while,
standing on the edge of the circle.
I didn't expect You to notice me.
I listened in for a short time.

Lord,
if You don't mind I'll move on ahead,
start journeying
with some of the more advanced disciples.
We know where You're heading,
it's great to be in the vanguard,
we can begin to be more Spirit led,
move more with the flow,
explore faith issues that create a challenge.
It's great to feel the freedom of the Spirit,
less restricted,
it allows movement at a different pace.
There is absolutely no point
in going over things
that you know already,
I'm sure You'll agree,
moving at the pace of the slowest
is so debilitating.

What was that You said Lord?
They are Your advanced disciples!
But I didn't see any one I knew,
no familiar faces,
in fact they were all children.
What was that,
of such is the Kingdom?

Written by Albert Bogle 2008

Commitment

Lord,
can I talk to You a bit more about commitment?
What exactly would You say
makes a good disciple?
I guess it's about
keeping the rules,
attending church every Sunday,
praying a lot,
keeping the ten commandments.
Is it actually true
that You once asked a guy
to sell up everything he owned
and give all the money he made to the poor?
That must have taken some nerve.
I mean,
to ask someone to sell all their possessions,
it gives a whole new meaning
to the idea of travelling light.

Some of Your ideas are challenging
to say the least:
turning the other cheek,
loving your enemies,
accepting strangers as neighbours.
You say it's not about rules and achieving,
nothing to do with rule keeping at all?
I find that strange.
I know some disciples that
are into rule keeping in a big way.
Have they got it wrong?

Lord,
could You explain this grace thing to me?
It all sounds too easy.
Live any way you want and God accepts you.
Ah, You say 'no' to that.
What do You mean?
You can only live one way,
the right way!
Because God accepts you.
Is it when we know God has accepted us
that we want to live a new way out of gratitude.
Ah, that's an interesting motivator.
Can we talk about this again?

Written by Albert Bogle 2008

Political

Excuse me Lord,
but with all this politicking
going on at Westminster
someone asked me what way You would vote?
It got me thinking.
Do You expect Your disciples
to get involved with politics?
Your first lot of disciples were into politics.
Judas was a right zealot.
He wanted You to declare UDI.
The apostles were a mixed bag.
The brothers James and John,
they wanted to be Your right hand men
when You took power.
I think they must have misread the signs.
They thought You were literally
standing for office.
Judas, was he really all about freedom fighting?
You know I think You nailed it when You said,
"render to Caesar what is Caesar's
and to God what is His."

Lord,
help me to make those distinctions more clearly,
give me the courage to stand up for the things
I know to be true and just.
If I have to protest,
help me do it because it is right.
Lord, help me to understand the power I have
when I clasp two hands together and say,
Father.
The more I pray, the more I protest
not simply with words, but with my life.

Lord, help me pray a life
and help me to live my prayers.
Now is that not pretty radical
or even political?

Written by Albert Bogle 2008

How long?

Look God,
how long is this going to last?
I'm just an insignificant player.
I feel You're putting all the blame on me.
It's got worse since I started following You.
Am I responsible for all that goes wrong
in the world?
I just have to live in the street beside the
bomber.
Everything gets pushed at me:
drugs,
knives,
alcohol,
pictures of dying babes,
information.
They tell me it's all too much.
I feel like a push button.
I'm on.
I'm off.
It's Your world, not mine,
I never even asked to be here!
Did I ask to be born?
So why are You treating me like this?
Why do I feel angry, disappointed, let down?
Time is ticking away.
Before long I'll be away.
What will I have done with my life?
Nothing!
And then You'll be mad with me.
Look I'm here,
protesting.
I'm asking You to look
at my situation
at my street
my town
my time
my life
my thoughts.
O God, do something.

Written by Albert Bogle 2009

iDisciples

Lord,
I've been thinking about
a catchy name for our group.
I've come up with iDisciple.
'Why?' You might ask.
Well 'i' stands for something that is
in touch
in tune
invaluable.
Modern, catchy and up to date.
There's the
iLife
iMac
iRiver and the iPod,
so why not the
iDisciple?

So what will the 'i' in disciple stand for?
Independent?
Irritable?
Intolerant?
Maybe it's more about
discipling the 'I'
that is so much at the centre of our lives,
helping us to become part of the inside track,
running closer to You.
Your word is all about information
helping us all become
relevant and smart
in a confused and changing world.
What was it You said?
'As wise as serpents and as harmless as doves.'
In other words You expect us to be
icons of Your image.
Now that's something for us all to imagine.
Think about it,
an iDisciple!

Written by Albert Bogle 2009

Discipleship diversions

Lord,
keeping focus isn't easy.
There are so many distractions on the way,
it's hard to keep my eye on You.
I don't want to look elsewhere
but there are so many voices,
different offers -
discipleship diversions
I call them.
I know the wrong relationships will hold me
back,
but sometimes it is so appealing,
just for once to think about myself,
my dreams, my life.
Doing the right thing all the time
is so demanding,
it's not feasible,
it gets lonely.
Sometimes I think I'm the only one following.
It feels like I'm in a wilderness.
Cut off.
Stranded.
Facing temptation.
Surrounded with stones.
Living in a hard place.
So what would I give for a bit of fame?
A bit of power?
A bit of recognition?
Turn stones into bread ?
Sell my soul to the devil?
Lord,
I think You've been here Yourself
I mean in my wilderness.
You passed this test long ago.
You couldn't be bought.
You couldn't be flattered.
You kept close to Your Father.
You listened to His Word
Lord, I'm listening,
I'm going to keep focused.

Written by Albert Bogle 2009

The plans

Lord,
so what's Your plan for my future,
You know, my life?
I read I think in Ephesians
that You have a lifetime of good works
set out for all of us.
A kind of to 'do list'
with our names at the top.
Look, I'm sorry I ask so many questions
but I do want to stay in Your will.
Can You explain this free will thing?
If You have a 'to do list' for me
do I have a choice?
Is it all pre-set, pre-planned,
You know pre-determined?
Like predestined?
And is that the same as fate?
If it's gonna happen, it's gonna happen?
Somehow I think there's more to all this
than I can grasp.
I'm living this life in time
and You're advising me from eternity.
Well, You're outside of time,
You're timeless!
Yet You've lived through our time experience.

Lord, I just want to know that I'm not a robot.
I do believe I've been made in Your image.
Now, if I'm in Your image
I must be free, free to think, free to live,
free to be, free to love.
I guess it's when I'm free and loving You
that I discover Your 'to do list'.
Lord, help me to stay close to You
and give me the grace and the charisma
to attract others into Your Kingdom,
to turn them around
and recognise Your
unconditional love.

Written by Albert Bogle 2009

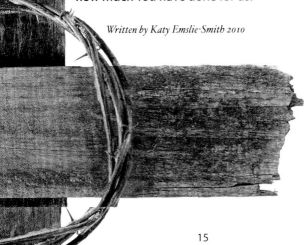

Lord of the cross

Jesus,
Lord of the cross,
forgive us our familiarity
and our forgetfulness.
We have made the cross familiar,
we have gilded it,
made it smooth and gold to handle and hang.
We have split it into the spectrum
of stained glass, to walk past,
week on week.
Forgetting,
crossing out,
that for You it was no smooth or beautiful
thing,
but bare splintered wood,
rough hewn by callous hands,
heavy and dug deep into open skin.
The stabbing crown,
made for your mocking,
nails, cold and sore, driven
through lonely hands held high,
still blessing.

Jesus,
Lord of the cross,
make us less familiar
with the suffering of the cross,
that we may remember again
how much You have done for us.

Written by Katy Emslie-Smith 2010

Why did she weep?

Jesus,
why did she weep?
This woman outside the circle,
outside convention,
unwanted, unclean, unloved,
the one whom You honoured,
in her dishonour,
by accepting her gift.
Did she know an early grief
as she poured the oil of mourning,
fragrancing the room with intimation of
death,
and matting her hair with the dust of the
road?
Or were they the tight tears of anger,
unruly outrage
to see You disrespected, ruled out of ritual?
No kiss for You, no water for Your feet,
no oil on Your head,
from the ones deeply learned in these ways
and shallow in love.
Or were they simply
the unstoppable tears of love,
cried from the broken place?
An ocean released by
the first touch of forgiveness?
Grief.
Anger.
Love.

I envy her emotion, Lord,
for we have captured the cross in cognition,
laid logical lines around it
and crossed out passion.
Release us, Lord, to sense again
the extravagant emotion
of forgiveness freshly known.

Written by Katy Emslie-Smith 2010

That's what Lent is about

Jesus,
sure, we can deny ourselves,
that's what Lent is about isn't it?
Giving up a bit of chocolate,
watching less television,
maybe giving more to charity.
We can handle that idea.
But losing our lives?
That is a bit extreme, don't You think?
Be reasonable,
we really would prefer it if You had
edited that part,
crossed it out of the text.
Don't get us wrong, Jesus,
we are happy to walk part of the way with
You,
shoulder a burden or two,
like Simon of Cyrene,
help out when You are in trouble.
But we really would like to
lay down the cross again
when we choose,
and go back to where we started.
That makes sense to us.

But You asked us to follow You for the full
journey,
no stopping off,
no looking back,
till in losing our life for You
we discover ourselves in the astonishment
of life found,
over and over and over,
abundant,
risen.

Written by Katy Emslie-Smith 2010

Questions

Jesus,
questions come,
honest, battling ones,
with each strike of the ten o'clock news –
Haiti, Helmand, Darfur –
when suffering asks of faith
can the cross speak love even here?
And Jesus, in the peppered hours
of the night, three in the morning,
the questions come,
when our fears for the future rattle:
the shadow on the x-ray,
the loom of dementia, old age.
When doubt asks of faith,
can the cross speak love even here?
Jesus, questions from the needy places,
You don't always answer directly,
but rather meet us with this –
that while we were broken, distant people
You died for us.
In suffering and doubt,
our powerless states,
easy answers would be too cheap.
Rather at Your cost
You allow us this rich discovery
of God's love shown.

Written by Katy Emslie-Smith 2010

Suffering servant

Suffering Servant,
You surprise us.
Without the cross,
we seek for power
in the noisy machinations
of a mechanistic world,
we handle rejection with retaliation
and try to stamp justice by wielding might,
courting popularity
in a quest for healing.

But You teach
that strength can lie in silence,
that weakness can be the cradle of courage,
that submission deflates violence of power,
that real justice never comes by force,
that Your rejection gives us acceptance,
that our peace comes from Your punishment,
that only Your wounds can truly heal
and that only Your innocent death
can give the guilty life.
Suffering Servant,
You surprise us.

Written by Katy Emslie-Smith 2010

It is finished

'It is finished':
Friday's worst and best news.
The darkest hour
when the grief of God
had riven the sunlight from the sky
and the cost of sin was seen
in the broken body of Jesus.
God dead, crossed out,
finished.

But the best news,
as in the brightness of Sunday morning,
of forgiveness found,
perfect, completed, fulfilled
unchangeable freedom.

Jesus, help us to grieve for our world
as in the darkness of Friday,
to spend ourselves for those
who live in the grey uncertainty of Saturday,
and to hope for our world
in the brightest light of Sunday.

Written by Katy Emslie-Smith 2010

The crucified poor

God Almighty!
I struggle with all this.
Help me to understand.
A man cried
seven phrases
in a dry hot dust covered desert.
Most thought he was mad
but his words changed humanity.
It seemed no one was listening
they were too hot to care,
everything was over exposed,
including their souls.

Too much sunlight obscures the view.
He cries 'I'm thirsty'.
He became invisible.
Nothing changes.
The crucified poor are left
thirsty today.

Written by Albert Bogle 2010

Saved by a prayer

Four phrases left,
still breathing hope.
He speaks a word
where hope is lost.
He hangs amidst a waste of space,
where a thief, and a murderer have graced
and something changed a selfish heart.
He empties out his
fearful thoughts.
He'd be forgotten,
lost in time,
forever damned
and then an echo to the thought returns:
not lost
but found
in Paradise.

Written by Albert Bogle 2010

Crucifixion hasn't changed

God of grace,
I find it hard to turn away.
A man had six words left,
six before he died,
surrounded by treachery,
lies and steel.
As soldiers stabbed his hand with nails
He drew the sting and spoke a word
that demons fear
and angels can't repeat
and hammered blows were cushioned
by the shock – the cry, 'Forgive'.
Nothing changes.
The crucified still forgive today
because He first lived a word.

Written by Albert Bogle 2010

God forsaken

O God, Your man
still cries out.
With the third cry comes a puzzle.
Why would God deny his double?
It's one thing friends denying friends
but how can God deny himself?
Rejected, lost, abandoned, divorced,
can it be the Trinity is broken?
Two against one
a shadow cast across a face
and then a thought,
could God be dead?
We're all alone on the edge of time.
Dying God forsaken,
crucified by our fathers.

Written by Albert Bogle 2010

I can't believe

I couldn't believe it, Lord,
but it still fills my mind:
the blood,
the lacerations,
the pain,
the loss.
You promised so much:
new life,
new hope,
a new way,
and on Your cross
I saw it all come to an end.
Just the same old brutalities,
the anguish so common already,
and death with all its familiar
sorrow
and grief
and finality.

I couldn't believe it, Lord,
but it still fills my mind;
my King of kings
with that crown of thorns
and stripped of all clothing
on a cross not a throne.
You promised so much:
healing,
life abundant,
love eternal.

Just the same old story,
of me on my own,
of darkness not light,
of weakness, not strength.
I still can't believe it, Lord.

Written by Members of
St. Matthew's Church, Perth 2010

Out of sight

A tomb so cold
for a body so rigid.
Out of sight, out of mind,
out of the way.

Yet You're not fully forgotten,
by me at least, Jesus,
for part of me is buried
in that tomb with You.

You took my pain
my sin
my foolishness
my self;
and You made me new
and helped me live
and brought me hope.

Is that hope gone now?
Are You gone too?
Where can I seek and find now?

Oh Eli, Eli lama sabachthani!
My God, my God
why have You forsaken me?
Come back to me, Lord.
Rise from the tomb, Lord.
Bring hope and love
and glory once more.

I need You every hour.
I need You every day.
I need You, oh I need You.

In Your tomb so cold,
with Your body so rigid
You're out of sight,
but in my mind.
My only way.

Written by Members of
St. Matthew's Church, Perth 2010

New day

Thank You, Lord, for this new day.
Every day is a gift.
I saw the sun rise
breaking up the night
and it felt warm on my face.
And this evening the sun will set
the darkness will return
and the air will chill,
and so it goes
day after day after day.

But each new day reminds me of a particular
new day,
the day Your Son rose
and He won't disappear beyond the horizon.
He rises up high
His light and warmth penetrate everywhere
and everything;
radiant,
life-giving,
warming my face,
my whole being,
my very human heart.
You give my day, today, its reason.
You fling my regrets of yesterday far, far away.
You fill my heart with hope for tomorrow.
He is risen!
He is alive!
Hurray!

Written by Members of
St. Matthew's Church, Perth 2010

27

Promise

It's spring.
I notice the world
waking up from its winter death
into colourful, musical life.
And again
I have journeyed
through the winter-time of Holy Week
feeling the pain
the loss
the tears wept until no tears remain,
the agonising 'Why?'
But then…
JOY!
And not just for a season
but forever!
The unbelievable,
the impossible, has really happened.
An empty tomb
burial clothes cast aside
no stink of death.
No, here is
resurrection,
the promise of new beginnings
and fresh starts,
the confirmation of love
that is without a limit,
the demonstration of the power of God
over and above everything else.
How great is our God!
Who else would have thought of it?

Written by Members of
St. Matthew's Church, Perth 2010

Nonsense talk

You know, He said He would rise again.
You know, it was written in the old scriptures
that He would rise again.
You know, it was His destiny to rise again.
And yet.

And yet.

And yet, it still seems a little too incredible.
Can it be true?
Do I want it to be true?
What does it mean if it's true?

I think I'll choose…
… to ignore it
… to see for myself
… to just believe it.

Why is it that I have trouble believing good
news?
Is it that nothing good ever happens to me?
Is it that I don't deserve good things to
happen to me?
Is it that I don't think God does good things
any more?

Today, Father,
help me to believe without seeing
to understand without explanation
to accept Your goodness with grace.

Written by Neil MacLennan 2010

Error 404

Error 404 – Resource Not Found
Sorry, the person you are looking cannot be found.
Perhaps it has been moved,
deleted or given new life.
Please try looking elsewhere,
or return to the place you came from.
If you think that you were directed here in error,
then please contact the source of your directions.

Uh-oh.
He was here three days ago.
How are we going to explain this one?
The tomb is solid, and the stone still seals it.
We thought there might be an issue here
…and there is.
I think I know what the answer is
but I don't like it.
And my overseers certainly won't like it.
Perhaps just best to keep my mouth shut.
I know the truth,
but my lips are as sealed as the tomb.
Wait.
Hang on there.
What did I just say?
'I know the truth'
I. Know. The. Truth.
I. Know. The. Truth.
I. Know. The. Truth.

Father,
however unbelievable this might seem to others,
I testify that I know the truth.
I may have difficulties and challenges
in all sort of areas
but I know the simple truth.
How reassuring, the truth, the whole truth
and nothing but the truth.
My lips are not sealed.
Help me to speak the truth boldly.

Written by Neil MacLennan 2010

The gardener God

I was looking for a man.
I looked where He last was, but I couldn't see Him.
I didn't know where to look next.
I was at the end of the road,
but I knew He must be somewhere,
I must keep looking.
Does anyone else know where He is?
What about you?
Or you?
Why are you all asking me the same question?
Why do you think I'm crying?
I'm upset.
Look,
I'm looking for my Lord.
I want to save Him.

You! Gardener! You must have seen something.
Did you see anyone take Him away?
Did you take Him away?
I'll not be angry, just tell me where He is.

For all my looking,
I never saw two angels.
For all my looking,
I never saw the folded grave clothes.
For all my looking,
I never saw my Lord.
WHY CAN'T I SEE WHAT'S IN FRONT OF ME?

It's not that I was lost, but that I was found.
It's not that I was looking,
but that I was being sought.
It's not that I said His name, but that He said mine.
Mary. Jim. Laura. Andrew. Karen. Robert…
Father, You speak my name,
let me take a moment to hear it in my mind.

Let me now see You wherever I look.
Let me see You in the wonder of creation.
Let me see You in the face of the poor,
the naked and the hungry.
Let me see You in the meditations of my heart,
the attitude of my mind
and the work of my hands.

Written by Neil MacLennan 2010

Poor Thomas

Poor Thomas,
not about when his pals met Jesus again.

Poor Thomas,
perhaps a little jealous that he wasn't there?

Poor Thomas,
wanted to see for himself.

Poor Thomas,
his name condemned in history as 'the doubter'.

Poor Thomas,
can you blame him?

Poor Thomas,
confronted by his boss.

Poor Thomas,
embarrassed in front of his friends.

Poor Thomas,
humbled by his God.

Thank you Thomas,
for the blessings from Jesus
to all who came after you.

Father, it's easy to mock Thomas,
but would we have done the same thing?

Forgive the times
we ask for the show-off miracle.

Forgive the times
we ask for selfish prayer.

Forgive the times
we demand an ultimatum.

Grant us a blessing
listening to the testimony of others.

Grant us a blessing
by obediently reading Your Word.

Grant us a blessing
simply by believing.

Grant us Your peace.

Written by Neil MacLennan 2010

Sorry, a bit late

Good morning, Lord,
I'm running a bit late.
Perhaps You can tell me why it is
I always seem to be the last to
see things,
accept things,
believe things?
The thing is
I want to believe,
but,
there is always that voice in my head.
You know, the one that always asks
the difficult questions.
I end up being
part of the awkward squad.
Even then,
I sort of believe.
It's a kind of strange feeling,
I can't just walk away,
I can't deny You.
The thing is,
I trust You.
I really do.
So does that mean
I believe?
Well it must mean I believe
in You!

Written by Albert Bogle 2010

The turn of a coin

Lord,
I've mentioned this to You before.
Remember,
I've already asked You about directions.
I know You spoke about
the way
the truth
and the life.
The truth is, Lord,
too often I don't know the truth,
even when I see it.
Walking the right path.
heading in the right direction,
knowing your chosen path in life,
it must feel good.
So, how do you know you're on the right road?
Lord,
living life can be a hard struggle.
Sometimes I can hardly move,
too many confident people all about me,
moving quickly,
going somewhere.
And me?
I'm full of self doubt,
always looking for a sign, checking the road map,
asking You questions.
Lord,
thank You for not giving up on me.
Thank You for listening to all my questions.
In a strange way, when I'm here with You,
I don't feel lost.
You always make me feel
it's alright to ask questions.
It's almost as though
it's how I am beginning to understand,
the way
the truth
and the life.
Perhaps faith and doubt
are two sides of the one coin.
Just for once Lord, when I spin it
can it land on faith?

Written by Albert Bogle 2010

Resurrection is not on the agenda

Lord,
there is something about us as people.
We change
when we become members of
groups,
committees,
assemblies.
We become part of a new identity,
we allow ourselves to be absorbed
into the projected psyche of the committee.
We begin to work from an agenda,
we take on the role of doubters,
we become part of the inquisition.
Often we take our collective responsibility
too far,
we don't appreciate enthusiastic people,
we try to keep everything balanced.
Within the experienced wisdom
of the committee
we become 'reasonable people'.

Lord,
forgive us when,
along with others,
we haven't seen the full picture.
We've ignored the voices of change,
we've presided over decline and death,
we've rejected rumours of renewal.
Lord,
the next time
the women come knocking
on our committee room door
shouting 'Resurrection'
will
You
waken
us
all
up?

Written by Albert Bogle 2010

Sorry Lord, we're so unreliable

Lord,
isn't it strange that
we humans can be
doubters one minute
and believers the next?
At the heart of all this doubting
is a fear we might be wrong,
we might be seen to have lived a lie.

Lord,
we must seem very unreliable friends.
We agree with You one minute,
we even make promises,
but we can change very quickly.
We're such a fickle bunch,
yet You don't give up on us.
You never seem to stop believing in us.
You make me feel ashamed.
You must have such courage to love,
to forgive,
to look vulnerable,
to embrace our doubt and still call us friends.

Lord,
I can't talk for the others
but I can talk for myself.
Help me to keep believing,
keep me faithful in all I say and do.
Forgive me when I cause others to doubt.
Forgive me when I have hurt You,
by my attitude,
by my actions,
by my lack of trust.
Today, standing in the light,
I address You as Lord
and even in my darkest moments of doubt
I still need to know You are my friend.

Written by Albert Bogle 2010

A touch of doubt

Lord,
here I am doubting again,
but it's a different kind of doubting.
I was just thinking,
what would I do
if I couldn't pay
the mortgage,
the car,
the utilities bill?
What would I do
if I lost my job,
lost my friends,
lost my memory?
Would I still talk to You?
Would I hide away from Your presence?
Lord,
I don't know how I would react.
Lord, I guess I'm a born worrier.
I want to pray for people who are in the above
situations.
Remind them You are their shelter,
draw close so they don't feel isolated,
bring into their lives a deep sense of Your
warmth and forgiveness,
draw their friends around,
remind them of Your constant love,
seek them out in their hiding place.
Lord, help me believe
You care about our everyday needs.
Give me the courage to look beyond our
doubting
to embrace hope,
to be grounded
in the knowledge of Your love,
believing all things work together for good.
Even my times of doubt.

Written by Albert Bogle 2010

37

Doubters anonymous

Lord,
I take heart when I see
You don't write off doubters like me.
I also take heart when I realise
Sarah, Abraham's wife,
she doubted,
she even smiled,
incredulously,
when she was told
she would have a child in old age.
Moses not only doubted
but argued his point with You
when You called him
to lead a group of slaves to freedom.
There was a whole group of Israelis,
a generation who lost the plot,
didn't believe.
But You never gave up on their children.
Oh and Elijah, that great pillar of faith!
When he had a nervous breakdown,
because he was afraid
hiding in a cave,
You taught him
that signs and wonder
speak to the novice.
But it's the 'still small voice'
that engages a determined disciple.
Lord,
I'm glad I can speak to You.
I'm amazed You listen.
You know I believe.
I often doubt because I want to believe.
I don't try to believe because I'm afraid to doubt.
Help me with my unbelief.

Written by Albert Bogle 2010

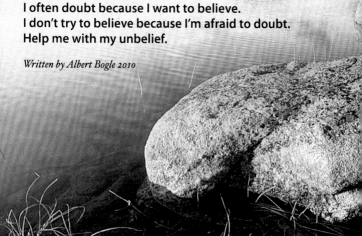

Work as worship

I'm thinking of the cross
and I humbly offer my life back to You, Lord.
You have done so much for me,
loved me so much,
but life is so busy with work,
it seems that work is all I have to offer You:
meeting people,
doing deals,
writing reports,
paperwork,
hard work,
setting up appointments,
filing,
email (endless email).
Holy Spirit, help me to offer all that I am
and all that I do as an offering to God.
So here I am Lord, laying my work before You
at the foot of the cross as an offering.
Giving over my whole week (not just Sunday)
to worship You.
Giving my ordinary every day life,
my sleeping, eating, going-to-work,
and walking-around life as an offering:
my emails,
my meetings,
my reports,
my work.
May they become
Your emails,
Your meetings,
Your reports,
Your work, Lord.
This week,
all week,
at work,
I am worshipping You Lord.

Written by Ruth Walker 2010

Valuing others

I'm thinking of the cross
and I can't begin to imagine how bad that was,
physically and emotionally,
Lord.
Betrayed, deserted, beaten, in agony.
And still You thought about others,
looked to their needs,
and made sure they were cared for.
They knew You valued them.
And here I am Lord,
concerned and hurt
about what might happen in re-organisation,
possible redundancy.
It's nothing compared to Your suffering
and yet I can only think about myself
and my needs.
What might happen to me?
Yet my colleagues are in the same position
and they are vulnerable, hurting.

Help me to lift my eyes from myself,
think about others and their needs:
to actively support them,
to see them through Your eyes,
to show them they are of value to me,
and to You,
to help them in practical ways where I can,
to pray for them too.
Thank you Lord that You value me,
I am resting in that thought.

Written by Ruth Walker 2010

The death of a colleague

I'm thinking of the cross
and what You did for me, Jesus,
how I have whole and lasting life.
I'm thinking as I sit in the church
at my colleague's funeral,
'Did I ever tell him about You?'
He knew I went to church,
but did I live as if my life
had been changed by You?
Did I show real interest in others,
value them, care for them?
Did I do my job in a way that was clear
I was serving You Lord?
He knew I was interested in You, God,
but did I ever speak to him about You,
how You were interested in him,
how You loved him enough
to send Jesus for him,
how believing in him
meant that death didn't need to mean
an end to life.
I'm thinking of the cross
and what You did for me Jesus,
how I have whole and lasting life.
I'm thinking of the cross
and what You did for my colleague.
Did he ever know
he could have whole and lasting life?
I'm thinking of the cross
and what You did for all those I work with.
Holy Spirit,
I'm asking for Your boldness and passion
to share with my colleagues
how they can have whole and lasting life.

Written by Ruth Walker 2010

Working with all my heart

I am thinking of the cross
and I am reminded again Lord
of how You loved me
with all Your heart,
gave up life for me,
so that I might live for You.
How can I not love You?
How can I not whole heartedly live for You?
So as I start off my working week Lord,
I commit to live and work
wholeheartedly for You in my job
and to serve You in my place of work.
Help me to remember that whatever I do,
it may be hard, or dull, or fantastic,
it's You God I'm serving first and foremost,
before company,
organisation
or boss.
You have placed me here for a purpose
to serve You.
So whatever I do,
whether it is setting targets,
managing expenses,
pitching for work,
working with people,
developing business plans,
chairing meetings,
writing e-mails,
I'll work at it with all my heart
for I am working for You Lord.

Written by Ruth Walker 2010

Feeling rejected

I'm thinking of the cross,
but I'm ashamed, Lord,
for it's a big black cross
that has been put through my work
that I am thinking about.
The boss doesn't like it,
doesn't like the ideas
I have offered in my report,
doesn't like the words I have used,
wants it changed – and by tomorrow.
I have spent hours working on it,
hours of my personal time,
my family time, my thinking time,
and all I see are crosses scoring out my work.
I thought it was brilliant!
Full of good ideas and innovations,
well argued, well written.
If the plans were adopted,
they could bring transformational change
to our business.
But the boss has other ideas
and I feel frustrated, hurt, foolish, abandoned,
lonely, tired, de-motivated, discouraged,
rejected.
Lord, I am thinking of the cross
and all that You did for me and for others
and my hurt is so small compared to that.
Lord, I am thinking of Your cross
and, how You love me and value me,
how You have plans for me.
So I am praying, Lord, You'll restore me,
encourage me, re-motivate me,
re-inspire me in faith and work!
To be more gracious in the way I respond,
and to achieve tomorrow's deadline.

Written by Ruth Walker 2010

Why this job?

I am thinking of the cross and how You, Lord,
the King, the Ruler of the entire world
were humble enough
to let people nail You to a cross
and die there for me.
You didn't want special privileges,
You weren't worried about Your status,
You had a hard job to do.
Here I am Lord in a pretty ordinary job,
with no prospect of promotion,
with little status or influence.
Every day I face a dull,
hard and daily grind of physical labour.
Why am I in this job Lord?
I feel insignificant to this company,
yet I long to be significant for You.
Help me to recognise
that You have placed me here,
to be Your representative.
Help me to be like 'salt and light' here
bringing out the God flavours in my workplace.
Help me to see the ordinary things I do,
the little things I am able to say
about my confidence in You,
may be eternally significant
for the people I meet each day.
Help me to be generous
in the way I treat my fellow workers
so that they will be prompted to open up to God.
Give me passion and pleasure,
I pray, for this ordinary, insignificant job
so that I may demonstrate the significance
of a life lived for Jesus.

Written by Ruth Walker 2010

Work – God wants the best for me!

I am thinking of the cross, Lord,
and how it represented
how much You loved people.
I am thinking of the cross, Lord,
and how it represents
Your love for me,
and I am resting on Your love.

I am thinking of the cross, Lord,
and how it represents
Your provision for me.
You value the sparrow
and You value me.
You want the best for the wild flowers
and You want the best for me.

I am resting in Your focus and attention,
so thank you that I have a job.
Thank you for the skills You have given me
so I can work well and play to my strengths.
Thank you that work provides me
the means to live and give.
Thank you that weekends mean
I can rest and be restored.
Thank you that You take pride in me
and what I do.
I feel truly blessed when I reflect on that.
Thank you that You love me wherever I am,
whatever I'm working at.
Thank you for work.

Written by Ruth Walker 2010

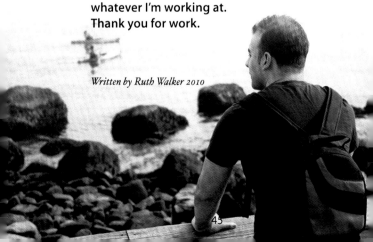

I'm not moving

Lord,
here I am,
drinking coffee,
feeling guilty,
with a thousand and one things still to do:
letters still to write,
decisions still to be made,
relationships still to mend,
deadlines to be met,
expectations to be fulfilled.
But I'm still here,
thinking about the cross shaped space.
I'm thinking about
the way I walked through the space.
I wanted to stay a while,
not move,
just stand there,
in the space,
living in the space,
working in the space,
praying in the space,
receiving your 'Spirit breath'.
I guess this is my time to reflect,
my prayer time.

Lord, I'm struggling in the cross shaped space.
Help me clear a space in my life
to spend with You,
to live in Your space,
Your space that allows me to receive forgiveness,
Your space that gives me grace to forgive others,
Your space that helps me become a servant.

Lord,
I want to stay in this space,
soak in this space,
laugh in this space,
dance in this space,
die in this space.
Lord thank you for the gift of faith
giving me courage to believe,
to know this is the right space
in which to be.

Written by Albert Bogle 2010

Your man in Havana?

Lord,
here I am,
once again,
walking through a hospital corridor.
It's strange, when you wear a clerical collar
most people put on their best smile,
they acknowledge your presence,
others give a nod.
It's almost as though
I'm recognized as Your man,
like 'our man in Havana'.
I wish I was 'Your man in hospital'.
Lord,
on the subject of healing,
I know it's one of the gifts of the Spirit.
Walking down this corridor
I wish I could reach out and see the sick
healed.
How wonderful that would be.
Yet You didn't heal everyone in an instant,
Your healing went deeper,
took longer,
cost nothing,
cost everything.
Lord,
help me understand,
what it means to pray with the sick,
to journey with those who will not improve,
to rejoice with those in remission,
to believe with those who believe,
to believe for those who struggle to believe,
to be Your man
bringing Heaven into this place,
this ward,
this corridor,
this place where people journey
in search of healing,
deeper healing.

Written by Albert Bogle 2010

Joy

Holy Spirit,
scent of Heaven,
where does joy come from?
It seems to be the fragrance of Heaven
caught in Your breeze.
Thank you for the moments
when joy has been mine,
when I have been surprised
by its presence,
or overwhelmed by its power.
Of all Your fruit,
this is one I long to know for myself
and for everyone I know.
Scent of Heaven,
show me how to be a gardener
in Your joy orchard today,
cultivating joy
in the life of others.

Written by Peter Gardner 2010

Patience

Holy Spirit,
presence of Christ,
I can't wait
for justice to roll,
for God's Kingdom to come,
for Christ's love to be known,
for all my prayers to be answered,
for true worship to begin,
for the people who slow everything down,
for those who are stuck in a rut,
for all who can't go at my pace.
I can't wait,
I can't wait on You.
Presence of Christ,
teach me the slow grown fruitfulness of
patience
that I might learn to wait on You
like a servant,
like a waiter,
like one who listens
and washes feet.

Written by Peter Gardner 2010

Peace

Holy Spirit,
fire of Pentecost,
kindle in me the desire for peace,
to see peace in this world,
among Your people,
within my family,
between my neighbours,
in this village, town or city,
between tribes, nations and powers.
Help me to look at a map
and see the places where peace has grown,
and rejoice that peace has been found,
like summer fruit found beside a path.
Fire of Pentecost,
warm my life today,
that I might become like a warm greenhouse
for growing peace,
where what I say and the way I say it,
what I do and refrain from doing
might produce a rich harvest of peace.

Written by Peter Gardner 2010

Goodness

Holy Spirit
living water,
Your fruit is perfect,
better than any we could buy
or grow by ourselves.
You grow goodness,
the fruit of Paradise.
It is hard to imagine goodness
where there are no mixed motives,
no doubtful compromises,
even Jesus hesitated to be called good.
Forgive me, if I have been cultivating lesser
fruit,
pouring my energies into other things,
getting caught up in things that seem good
but are of little value.
Living water,
wash me clean,
clear my vision,
so that I can see the fruit You ripen
on my branches,
and tend the goodness
that You are growing
in and through me.

Written by Peter Gardner 2010

Kindness and gentleness

Holy Spirit,
breath of Heaven,
as gentle as a summer breeze,
how easily I am swayed in Your breeze.
Yet I get caught up in this world's ways,
impressed by strength,
decisiveness, determination,
leadership that powers ahead,
that makes a difference and is effective.
And all the time, like an expert gardener
You have been ripening other fruits,
that are undervalued and neglected
because they are soft and meek.
You grow kindness and gentleness
because they have the sweetest taste
and are most precious to God.
Breath of Heaven,
train me today to bear these precious fruits,
kindness and gentleness,
through all I say and plan and do.

Written by Peter Gardner 2010

Self-control

Holy Spirit,
wind of God,
I am inspired by the thought of Your freedom,
like the wind blowing wherever,
so spontaneous,
so new born,
so much fun.
I want to be like that, free!
Yet You grow self-control in me,
which seems so boring,
steady, predictable,
hard work, disciplined.
It reminds me of Jesus' call
to be his disciples.
Wind of God,
bend my will
and shape my desires today
so that I can choose
to follow Christ
always.

Written by Peter Gardner 2010

The teacher

Holy Spirit,
who perfectly knows the Father and the Son,
do Your enlightening work
and fill our minds with our God.
Education is wasted on the young.
It is only when we grow,
that we treasure every opportunity to learn.
There is so much we need to learn,
even after days, or months, or years,
of worshipping, praying, Bible reading,
faithful discipleship,
so much we still need to learn.
Our God is a great big God,
our Saviour's love is deep and wide,
and we are playing at the edges.
Holy Spirit, like our best teacher,
our most patient tutor,
take us by our hands,
lead us slowly but surely,
one step after another,
into a knowing of God,
through all the words He has spoken for us.
We need to learn these lessons,
not to earn salvation, not to earn God's love,
but that we might follow faithfully,
that we might have words to share.
Holy Spirit,
make learning fun for us,
each new day,
a new lesson of Christ
that we might grow in Him.

Written by Gordon Kennedy 2010

The liberator

Holy Spirit, life giving breath of God,
do Your powerful work
and make us alive in our God.
Holy Spirit, in what state did You find us?
Not many were strong,
healthy, fit, able, alive to God.
Too many were weak,
frail, condemned, defeated,
dead to everything.
Holy Spirit,
death cannot endure Your presence,
You are the breath of life,
that forever overwhelms death.
That our sin has condemned us to death,
You can overcome in us.
The victory of Christ,
the freedom of new life,
are made real in our lives
by Your powerful work.
You don't free us from the death of sin
to live only as we have already lived.
You bring us into the wide places of grace.
This is where we want to live,
alive to God, alive in Christ,
alive through Your power.
From life's first cry,
to our final breath,
set us free in Christ.
Holy Spirit,
keep us free.
When our enemy tries to snatch us back,
powerfully hold us in Your hand.
Set our feet on solid ground,
to stand in Christ,
and continue to stand.

Written by Gordon Kennedy 2010

The guide

Holy Spirit, who knows the way to God,
do Your needful work
and lead us from a far place back to our God.
I thought I knew the way,
not the rocky path,
but the green meadow alongside.
It was easy on my feet,
more pleasant for my eyes,
more fragrant for my senses,
It was a good way,
I thought it led to God.
But I was wrong.
Just a slight angle and over time,
this green way diverged from God's way,
until I was lost,
and not only lost, in deep trouble.
Suddenly surrounded by tempting sights,
enticing sounds, arousing aromas,
too hard to resist, they become a pit of hell,
and I fell in.

Holy Spirit, You know the way,
the right way.
The way You would guide me in,
might not be soft on my feet,
but it is true,
might not appear pleasant or fragrant,
but it leads to God.
Take my hand, don't let it go.
When I wriggle and struggle
You hold tighter.
When I break free,
You run after me,
carry me until I'm ready to be guided by You.
Powerful Spirit,
be a powerful guide
in the needful way.
Humble my proud spirit
to be led in Your way.

Written by Gordon Kennedy 2010

Loose talk

Today Lord,
I start again.
Help me to guard my lips.
No loose talk.
No put downs.
Help me listen to the rhythm of life
created by You
and play my part in time.
Give me discernment;
to know when to speak
to know when to be silent.
Give me insight
to move around the obstinate,
courage to hold ground when needed
and wisdom to know when to retreat.

Today Lord
I start again
making my moves
in the cross
shaped
space.

Written by Albert Bogle 2010

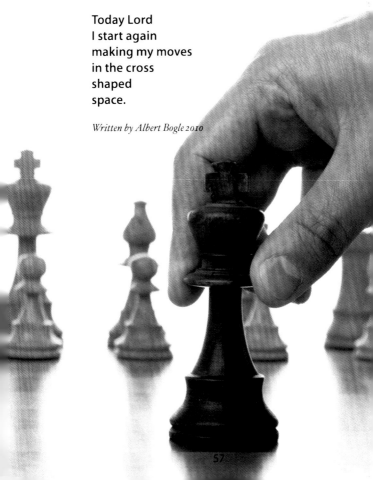

All my days

Creator God,
creating every week.
God of every weekday
creating and re-creating every day,
give strength to those who feel weak today.
God of the good days,
God of the bad days,
God of the troubled days,
God of the boring days,
God of the weary days,
God of the lazy days,
God of the war days,
God of the peace days,
God of the summer days,
God of the winter days,
give courage to all
who choose to live through these,
Your days.

God of every Tuesday,
God of this Tuesday,
God of the after,
God of the noon,
God of the afternoon,
God of the Tuesday afternoon,
God of the day off,
God of the off-day,
God of the cross,
God of the road,
God of the crossroad,
here I choose
faith today.

Written by Albert Bogle 2010

View from the cross

Lord,
standing in this space
I feel Your compassion protecting me
I see the darkness all around
I hear the noise of Your crucifixion
I fear that truth is silenced.
Standing in this space
I'm called to be
Your servant,
Your disciple:
to see,
to hear,
to speak,
to be crucified.
I'm overwhelmed by this darkness,
the silent pain of the abused child,
the tortured pain
of the manipulated teenager,
the defacing shame of a battered love,
the motionless anguish of a broken marriage,
the empty response of a lost memory,
the weary moment of a dying love.
In this space, Lord,
protect them with Your compassion,
gather them in,
gather them all in to Your
outstretched arms,
for in this cross shaped space
the wood and the nails are gone.
This is resurrection ground!

Written by Albert Bogle 2010

I don't fit in

Lord,
You know everything,
You know why
I can't go to church.
The pews are too well polished
the stained glass is too attractive
it has coloured my outlook for too long.
Actually,
everything is too well organised,
something is missing.
I think it is – the point.
Yes, the point is missing.
The sharp bit.
The jaggy bit.
The bit that pricks my conscience.

Lord,
I want a messy church
one that makes mistakes
one where I can belong
one where a person
like me can serve.

Lord,
I want to be part of church.
Answer me.
Help me find a place where
I can be
of use
to You and others.

Written by Albert Bogle 2010

Chill out

Dear Lord,
this is Sunday.
Help me keep it special,
different from all the rest.
Slow me down today,
let me feel Your presence
as I move through each hour.
I want to walk at Your pace,
discover Your path
and walk in it.

Lord,
I'm listening for Your word
I'm looking for the signs.
Draw near to me,
reassure my restless heart,
let me receive Your peace today.

Written by Albert Bogle 2010